A Boy and His Dream

A Boy and His Dream

and His

Ambrose Okosun

A BOY AND HIS DREAM

iUniverse books may be ordered through booksellers or by contacting:

iUniverse
1663 Liberty Drive
Bloomington, IN 47403
www.iuniverse.com
1-800-Authors (1-800-288-4677)

Because of the dynamic nature of the Internet, any web addresses or links contained in this book may have changed since publication and may no longer be valid. The views expressed in this work are solely those of the author and do not necessarily reflect the views of the publisher, and the publisher hereby disclaims any responsibility for them.

Any people depicted in stock imagery provided by Thinkstock are models, and such images are being used for illustrative purposes only. Certain stock imagery © Thinkstock.

ISBN: 978-1-4917-6755-9 (sc)
ISBN: 978-1-4917-6758-0 (e)

Library of Congress Control Number: 2015909478

Print information available on the last page.

iUniverse rev. date: 07/23/2015

This book is dedicated to GOD first and to my
Mother - Christiana and My Grandmother - Awanle. Without their
guidance and experience I would not be the man I am today.

To my son Osajie and my Daughter Joy who are the loves of my life.

Contents

Intro

IT CAN BE SAID THAT some people are truly dealt a bad hand in life. Some folks seem to have the best of everything practically handed to them. While others work their lives away just trying to stay afloat and try to be somewhat stable in life. Then there are those, who no matter what life throws at them they are able to rise to the occasion and conquer the issue at hand. It takes a special type of individual to do this. Most people would see the fear in trying to accomplish something that was said to be impossible for them. But to rise above and continue fighting for your dream, that speaks volumes about one's personal strength.

To be able to look beyond that and see what dreams you would reach if you could just make it through, is an entirely different world. A world, that most of us do not take the time to ever seek out. If everyone around you is doing their best just to maintain what they already have in life, who are you to think you can achieve more? What makes you think that you are any different than any of these other people that go on day by day in a monotonous world of doing the same thing every day for the rest of their lives? It is the fact that you realize that there is so much more to life than being eternalized in a rut when you have so much greater potential to seek out and maybe, just maybe leave a positive impact on this world before the end of your own time.

What if you were born into a less than ideal situation? We are all here as a result of two people. One being your Mother, and the other your Father. Not always do these two play their traditional roles in our lives. However, it is true that their gene pools have to come together in order to create another and it goes a little something like this.

On March 15th in the year of 1973 it was the night that the stars must have shined themselves a little bit brighter. In the small town of Lekki, Delta in Nigeria a beautiful baby boy is born. They named him Ambrose and he was a healthy addition to the beginning of a family.

However, short lived, while I was beginning my life, my parent's marriage was ending. It was found out that my father was already married to a woman before meeting my mother. Which was common practice in Nigeria. When it was learned that he had a family elsewhere, my maternal grandfather forced my mom to leave him and move back into the village. My mother didn't have any other choice. Here she was a new mother with a marriage based on lies. They divorced when I was only three months old. She quit her job to move back to the village and was struggling emotionally and financially and wasn't getting much support from anyone. Moving back to the village was the biggest mistake she would ever make.

Two years later my mother met a primary school teacher named Paul Duke, who was living in the same town as her. They started dating and were married 18 months later. Once my mother married, her new husband was promoted and they moved to another town far away. I was left to stay with my grandparents. Even though I now had a stepfather, my grandfather continually demeaned any thoughts of my birth father. The fact that he never liked people from Soweto town, the city where my father was from, was just the beginning of his insults. My maternal grandfather was the chief in his village. He had control over how things should function, who runs whom and what not. His name was Oba of Eki town. He was a spiritual man but used to worship a God called Ela. He would make me go with him until I became older and chose Christianity for myself.

Even though I was little I really didn't like the idea of my mother living someplace different than I. I was only five years old when she married my stepfather, the school teacher. I was mad at him for taking my mother so far away from me. I knew already that I would be disconnected from her. I missed her more than you could ever imagine and I longed for her to be with me again.

My maternal grandmother and uncles on that side of the family would forbid me to see my birth father. They would tell me that he was a loser, reckless, and a self-centered narcissist. One particular half-brother of my mothers, would tell me how horrible it was that my father had a fantastic job and was successful and that I was in a faraway village struggling. He said that I should be in the urban city with my father where there would be more opportunities for me. However he didn't realize that my father's first wife, who was my stepmother, would never let me experience a future so bright.

Here begins the story of my struggle, the story of my life, the story of all the things I have had to overcome.

And so it begins...

HAVE YOU EVER GONE TO bed hungry? You couldn't quite sleep because the pain from your stomach of being empty, was far too strong for you to escape. Your thoughts consumed completely by the need to feed yourself. All you can do is lie awake hoping it could just go away and let you sleep. As a boy very young it was hard to conceive why this was happening to me. But little did I know this was a part of the plan of the survival mode that I would need, in order to survive later in my life. God is good and works in mysterious ways.

Now, imagine this is your everyday. We all know that we need food to survive. It's what makes our bodies strong enough to go on. It's what lets us be mentally competent to handle and complete even the simplest of tasks. Sometimes we were only having one square meal a day and would drink more water to fill our stomachs. Again the strategy at the time that was needed to make ends meet.

My Uncle would say things about how I shouldn't be left suffering in this poor village, when I had a well off father like mine. He was right, but at the time I had no choice. I was just a young boy trying to survive. Life was different in Nigeria. My maternal grandfather was married to seven wives and four concubines. In certain societies such as Eki town, a woman could be contracted to a man as a secondary wife. Often having few legal rights and low social status in the community. As a result of this practice, I now have over

1

seventy-five cousins and I haven't even met half of them. My goal one day is to meet and greet them all and get some type of realistic value as to why all this was so necessary, or was it based on cultural exchanges and the cycle had not been broken.

My grandfather was the chief of his village. Yet his only source of income was from farming, which paid at peasant rates. There was no way he would ever be able to take care of all of his responsibilities through his income. That really left for all the wives to take care of the children. Each wife had up to seven or eight children, which then turned into survival of the fittest. As the wives began outcasting those children that were not desired or wanted, here is where my struggle began.

As a child growing up with my grandmother, there never seemed to be enough food. Of my grandfather's seven wives, my grandmother was number five, and almost the last in rank. In polygamous circles, a secondary wife is inferior in rank and treated just like that. With her being as they say 'lower on the totem pole', she was further down in line when it came to the necessities. Polygamous families share food, supplies and anything else of value.

By the time it was my grandmother's turn, she was often left with nothing. If anything, it would only be leftovers and crumbs. I was always terribly saddened that there was no food to eat. My grandmother continued to accept all the misfortunes and suffering that came her way. She was a remarkable woman in that she had hope. She had the hope that made her continue on in search of a better tomorrow.

Sometimes we would have just one meal a day. We would try to drink more water, if we had extra to supplement for our lack of food. Times seemed very primitive compared to current days. Mind you, this was all happening in the 80's and in Nigeria. Back then we were even using lamps as we had no electricity. There wasn't any electricity yet or an actual water supply. The only available water source was a nearby river in the next village. That would seem not nearly as awful as it really was. Until you realize that the next village was about 25 kilometers, roughly 15.5 miles away. A distance that even a person that was well nourished and healthy would consider strenuous. Again, fit of the fittest.

I was a young boy that was weak from hunger. Lacking nurturing from an adult and hesitant to accept any type of affection as I didn't know what this was. I would take my two gallon container, while my grandmother would take about a twenty-five gallon reservoir to fill in the water. We would walk barefoot to fetch the water. I remember it was dingy and unclean. We would bottle it up and take it back the same distance we had come. We were responsible for bringing all the water needed for my grandfather the chief, because he was entitled to food, water and clothing, as well as enough water for the rest of the household. Only then would we have water for home consumption. The only thing that saved me from voicing my opinion was the fact that I was a child at the time.

After the trek to retrieve the water, my grandmother would prepare our popular meal for the evening. We would eat boiled yam with red palm oil. I would continuously eat carbohydrates because they were the only food source available. I couldn't figure out what foods were nutritious and which were not. I didn't have the awareness to seek out healthy food. It is pure amazement that I somehow escaped malnourishment. The fact of the matter is that I very well could have been malnourished, but not having the availability of visiting a Doctor, it was never told to me.

There would be times where I would be absolutely starved. I would cry my eyes out in secret. I never wanted my grandmother to know how upset I had become. Mostly, because it would only add to her emotional distress and as a child I was very much attuned to how she was feeling. I felt terrible. There was no food, no appropriate housing, no clothing, and the supplies were very low. They treated me as an outsider, and no one ever had adequate supplies because that was just how it was back in the day. Which made me just another mouth that they had to feed which was an overwhelming struggle.

She did her best to keep me fed and clothed. What we were doing wasn't living, we were just trying to survive. Most days I would dress in a pair of torn pants and a shirt and no shoes. On other days pants and no shirt. Sometimes even just a shirt and no pants. Clothing wasn't important, feeding was. It's difficult to live each day going to sleep hungry and waking up the same, and having to start the day out all over wondering where you were going to find the ability or stamina to continue another day. When would it all end?

It was difficult to have a complete outfit as resources were very limited. I was very disturbed by this situation and this also prevented me from starting school early. This later was said to have affected my academic reasoning and functionalities. However, I always found a way to compensate. I was always sharing clothing with my other relatives. It was first come, first served. I don't remember ever receiving something brand new, while I was growing up. My clothing had already lived entire lives before it had finally reached my body.

As the hunger pains became unbearable, I would sometimes go to our neighbors for meals. While often they would hide what they had, because they too were rationing. Back at home my grandfather's concubines would take turns cooking for him. With him being the chief of the village, you would wait for grandfather to finish eating, and then go check to see if by some chance there would be some leftover scraps. It was like real life survival of the fittest. I'm still unsure how I was able to escape succumbing to malnourishment. God is good.

There were other children where I grew up. One day my grandmother sent me out to buy some seasoning to make soup. This little girl followed me into the alley and began pushing me. She kept pushing me further and further. She was confronting me and at the time I wasn't too sure as to why. She was much bigger than I and I was just a young boy. I was afraid. She pushed me and I hit my head, my skull seemed to split open, which scared her and she ran off. It still gives me chills today.

As I grew older, I was already stronger. Mentally and getting physically stronger. I was able to strategize. Your age in the family determined which privileges you would be allowed. The older you are the further you will get. I was the youngest which often left me behind. I remember vividly walking miles upon miles barefoot looking for relatives to visit so that I could eat.

On the day of the local market I would go to help out the vendors set up and sell. By doing this and helping them load their produce, I would get paid. This became a lucrative business and increased my great survival skills. I was finally able to begin earning for my future. This only fueled my ambitions in life and made me realize that I could reach my dreams if only I worked hard enough.

How I came to be

MY GRANDMOTHER WOULD CALL ME by my traditional name, "Aigbimeona". Which translates to the word untouchable in English. As time went on, how true this would be. She would always encourage me and tell me that she knows I will be great one day, and be a man of my own.

One day she had gotten sick, however, later we would find that she had been sick for sometime before she let anyone know. She was taken away to an urban city called Warri. At that time there was a lack of adequate treatment and awareness. She was sick for over a year and at the time I was taken to live with my mother until my grandmother could return. I was 7 years old. I was praying always so hard for her to be alright, to be able to come home. She was only 58 years old. It was then that my grandmother passed away. I was shattered. My heart was torn to pieces, as I lost hope and the will to survive. She was the only person that ever supported me and showed me love and affection and encouraged me to keep going.

There are so many things about my grandmother that seem to keep her memory alive. Such as this special soup she made that was called ogbono soup, which, I really enjoyed back then and still like to eat when I have the chance now. I missed everything about her. From her powdery hugs, to the treats she would bake, the grape juice she would make by herself, her understanding of me and most of all her sweet voice. She was the greatest lady in my life and she was taken away so suddenly.

I was very close to my grandmother. We used to do everything together. In doing things together she also was teaching me life skills. We would go to a local farm and fetch wood for the cooking fire. My grandmother wouldn't allow me to cut the trees myself and preferred to do it herself for safety reasons. I was a young boy yet and she was more experienced in how to do it properly. She told me of a story of a young teenager in the community that passed away from the same wood falling process. Grandmother said that the teenager ran towards the direction of the fallen wood, rather than away and was hit by the tree. The girl was pronounced dead on the spot.

Eventually my grandmother taught me how to safely fall the trees. She was very informative and had the patience to take the time to explain everything so that I could understand. She then allowed me to begin cutting up the wood myself. It was around this time that she developed throat cancer.

Growing up as an abandoned child I had to teach myself the things that my mother should have taught me. That or rely on other adults to take the time to teach me things that naturally are taught to you as you grow up. I used to go to bed and wet the bed at night. I would wake up shocked and ashamed. My grandmother wouldn't tell anyone about it hoping that one day I would outgrow it. Even if I would go use the bathroom to relieve myself before going to sleep at night, I would still wake up covered in urine. This happened because I was never truly potty trained. I had to teach myself in order to stop the behavior. Imagine being a young boy and not understanding why you don't have control over your bladder and wetting yourself. I had no one to ask.

One day one of our cousins came to visit us in the village. I was two years older than my visiting cousin. We both slept in the same clay bed together that was covered in a handmade crafted mat made out of palm tree leaves. I would wet the bed and then my little cousin rolled into it. When I woke up first I would make it look like he did it. At the time I thought it was funny and it helped me to make it through. It is the memories of how she cared for me even when no one else seemed to care that made me realize just how important she was in my life.

The worst part of losing someone that was so close to me is that it left a huge hole in my heart. It seemed as though the only person that had loved me and even remotely cared for me had left me to fend for myself in this ugly world. It left me with a huge abandonment issue that I carry to this day. Knowing that she had lived a full and happy life did not ease my grief whatsoever. It is not those who have died who are in pain, it is those who are left behind who truly suffer. I couldn't live without her. I felt that no one could love and truly care for me the way that she did. It was true, real, unconditional love. And believe me that is hard to come by.

The worst part of it is that her cancer was completely treatable. If she would have had access to doctors and treatments she could still be alive and well today. I can only imagine the joy she would have in being around my children here and still a huge part of my life.

Moving On

WITH MY GRANDMOTHER'S PASSING I was sent to move in with my mother and her husband in a town called Imo city, where they both lived. My uncle came with my mother and me, into a taxi to help me move. I didn't have many belongings to travel along with so it was easy to just pick me up and move. It took between two and three hours for us to make it to the place where my mother was living. All I was wanting was a good meal and a place to sleep. That, and I wanted to be secure.

I didn't really like the idea of moving in with them. Mostly because my mother's husband was living in a polygamous family and married to two wives. My mother was considered the junior wife in this arrangement. The situation was awful. None of the parties involved were happy with this arrangement and this affected me negatively. They would treat me with disrespect and very nasty and never considered me to be part of the family.

I had left my friends behind in the village where I had lived with my grandmother. Just because you are young and small doesn't mean that you don't have friends already at that age to lose. I could feel the change involved in moving before it ever even happened. And I knew it was not a change that would be for the better for me. Since I was already accustomed to abandonment I didn't really understand the feelings of missing or loving someone.

I don't blame any one of them. What person out there would willingly want to share their partner with another person, and then in addition that other person's child from a previous relationship? The first wife seemed jealous of both me, and my mother. One day a threat was made onto my mother and me, we were told to leave my stepfather. The threat came from another wife at that time. There was a daily fight for territory that made all of our lives a living hell. I hated the environment that I lived in, even at a young age.

I used to raise chickens. I would buy the chicks, raise them and then finally sell them when mature. It was a small business that was helping me to save some money. One day, my stepfather's other wife within the household came out and walked up to one of my chickens and split its head with an axe intentionally killing my chicken instantly. I remembered crying my eyes out that day. Trying to figure out how someone could just go ahead and do that. She was hateful and was very mean. I hated that woman with a passion, but eventually forgave her as my mother directed me to do. She did it to show that she had the power to make my life a living hell.

My mother later enrolled me at a local primary school. There was only one in town and that is the one I was sent to. From the beginning it was rough and I faced many challenges. First I had to learn the local language, because they didn't speak the same language as my grandmother's village. I had to survive and try to make new friends. My classmates used to bully me because I was the new kid and I didn't speak like them.

They normally would bully new students and take advantage of them. I wasn't prepared to take this torture from them so I began to come up with an alternative plan. One day on my way home from school, one of the boys that lived opposite of me along with his friends decided that they wanted to beat me while the others watched. I wanted to run, but I didn't because I realized if I ran the bullying would never stop. So I decided to man up and fight.

When I approached the spot where the boy and his gang were waiting for me, I summoned all the courage I had inside of me. The boy ran towards me hoping to beat me up on the spot. I waited and as soon as he reached me I bent over and picked him up high and he landed on the ground. I then proceeded to punch him and defend myself. While this was going on his gang was watching and laughing. The next day that very boy became my first friend at the school. From that point on the bullying stopped but it took me awhile to redeem myself because of fear.

While I was attending primary school I would always complete two additional assignments daily after school .One for my Stepfather and one for my Mother, so that we could survive. My Stepfather would become very angry if I didn't complete my assignment for him. After school each day I would go to my Stepfather's farm to help maintain the crops by weeding, tilling the soil, transplanting crops and cultivation in general.

My Stepfather also had three children of his own from his first wife. We were close in age but they weren't made to work on the farm, which nobody questioned until this time. Upon my return from the farm I would then help my mother to hawk. Hawking is selling a special Nigerian delicacy out of tropical sweet corn. There is quite a process that goes into making this dish. However, the results are well worth all the work it takes to make it.

First you harvest the dried corn. Then you separate the seeds from the stems and soak in hot water for two days. After two days you take the soaked corn to the processing machine. The machine acts similar to a blender in that it will make the material into a smooth substance. From there you pour it into a hot metal pot and stir it until it coagulates and finishes cooking. At this point you spoon the substance into a leaf and wrap it up to sell to customers for consumption. This was how I helped support my mother in order to pay for my primary school tuition fees.

My homework suffered at this time because I wasn't keeping up with it due to all of my other responsibilities. I was always very tired after these tasks, but I dare not refuse to accomplish the tasks assigned to me. I would have been thrown out of the house. This was the beginning of what others call overachieving. I always pushed and gave the 180% that was expected until it finally became a way of life and even at a young age, this was instilled in me, however, at the time I had no idea this is what was then, the beginning - of what would later be a lifestyle for me.

Figuring out my destiny

W E ARE ALL SHAPED BY experiences in our lives. Throughout experiences and events we are taught just how our lives will take form. I was living by trial and error.

Most children today are taught from infancy on how to respect and take care of their bodies. Just how you teach a toddler how to recognize when they need to use the restroom and when they do not, you are surely teaching them to realize clues that our own bodies give us. I was never taught that. I had to teach myself general hygiene, such as bathing, brushing my teeth and how to carry myself in public.

My mother did her best to raise me up right and to keep me God fearing. But I truly was surrounded by a bunch of women. I did not have any male role models in my life to help teach me the "boy" things that I desperately felt I needed to know. I never had a male figure who focused his time or effort on me. I lived day by day. All I could see then was what I accepted. Not knowing that one day it would become a life learning skill to survival and I would be able to adapt to whatever environment I was placed in.

We went to church every Sunday. My mother would often tell us not to make the same mistakes that she made. At the time of her meeting of my birth father she was attending nursing school. She truly wanted to make her own life better and be able to do things on her own before she met him.

It was only after I was born that the truth of my father's other family came out. From there my mother divorced and was basically returned to her village. Tradition held in that once divorced she was viewed as being useless. That home was the only place that would still accept you.

The best advice that my mother ever gave me is that I should never let others control my destiny. Perhaps she intended it as a warning for me to heed or something of that nature. Whatever her intentions were it has definitely stuck with me over the years. It has continued to motivate me through a great deal of decisions. It has pushed me to strive to be successful regardless of the obstacles and challenges that stood in my way, growing up. No one was going to control my destiny besides myself. I live by that philosophy today and is sustains me everyday.

I learned most of my skills by trial and error, as well as by watching others and then teaching myself. I would pick up the good morals and leave the bad, just as I did in church. And most importantly I knew the importance of not being one of those people that would lie. I was able to learn how to farm, weed gardens, run errands, do laundry and cook. I also knew how to keep the house clean and swept.

When you are born into a body that has just been considered an extension of yourself without any guidance, how would you even begin to know what it is all capable of? And you surely wouldn't understand the concept of people touching you that should already know not to.

When I was touched inappropriately by an older female family member, I didn't realize the severity of it all. I didn't realize what had truly happened, other than I knew it was wrong. I did notice that after that, my behavior changed. This person had unknowing to me, exposed me to adult consensual behavior, before I was mature enough to realize what was really happening. It only happened once and thankfully it never happened again after that one time.

While alone in the kitchen one day, this older female asked me to remove my pants. Then she began touching my private parts. I still remember vividly how she had me lay on my back on the kitchen floor, while she squatted on top of me. After a reasonable amount of time, which seemed like hours upon hours had passed, she stood up and asked me to put my pants back on. All I felt was shame.

From there we went back into the living room and joined the rest of the families. The kitchen was detached from the main house which made it easier for her to get away with it without the others knowing. She made sure to warn me not to tell anyone, or that she would be sure to hurt me. I was confused by it all and after that I was scared.

Sometime later in life, I tried it on another girl that was my neighbor and my age. At that time I was fifteen and should have enjoyed the feelings of experimenting with a peer of the opposite gender, but instead all I felt was that I had been previously violated. Without having a male role model it was difficult growing up and trying to figure out what was expected of me, being a male.

I wish someone would have taught me how to feel, how to love someone, how to respond to someone's love. How to actually love someone and how to know when someone does not have your best interest at heart. Still this day I do not know how to differentiate between the two. I hope to one day find the true meaning of happiness and how to love unconditionally and accept love from someone who truly has my best interest at heart.

Trying to make it all work

RELATIONSHIPS NEVER CAME EASY FOR me. First there was my mother's broken marriage to my father. Then my grandparents' where my grandmother did not seem to be loved nor was she respected. The final straw seemed to be the violation that had taken place on my own body. How was I to see past all this hurt and believe that this thing called love was actually possible. I struggle with this everyday.

How I longed to love and to be loved. How I tried to grasp what had happened to me when I could barely stand to try and process it all. I would try but it would just make me hurt. I hurt deeply inside both mentally/emotionally and physically. I wanted to be in a relationship because I felt that I needed to know what love was about. I thought that if you dated a woman and felt commonalities, that I would equate this to being in love. That and I wanted a family of my own, since I never had one growing up. This was so important to me. Later I would find that without love, having relationships and marrying someone would not pan out.

My relationship with this person after the incident was extremely distant. I avoided her as much as possible. It wasn't long after my grandmother passed away that I was then sent to live in a faraway town with my mother and stepfather. That was the last time that I saw this person alive. She moved on with herself and ended up getting married and having two children.

Later in my life, she passed away during child bearing while trying to have her third child. We didn't actually see eye to eye to talking about the incident and I never took the chance to confront her as to what she did. By the time that I was actually mature enough to have the conversation she had already passed away. I never spoke of this to my family. I was either too scared or too ashamed. It embarrassed me that I was so easily taken advantage of. Even though I was just a young boy. It affects me to this day, but I go on.

Looking back, my fear mostly stemmed from thinking that my family would not believe me. Inside I wanted to tell someone but could never summon up the courage to do so. God rest her soul although I don't believe that I truly ever have forgiven her. I will continue to work on this until one day the bond of that devastating act – which affects relationships that I have had then and now – will always be affected. I know I must let it go, but this will have to be when I truly can lift that burden and let it go.

It was only later that I realized that I had fallen victim to a heinous crime. My innocence was taken from me at such an early age. Then there was the guilt that was inside of me that this was all somehow my fault. It ate away at my self-esteem daily. Depression also found its way to me. I was tormented by it. My mind could not escape it. Then came the anger. I was angry at my cousin for doing this to me. Surely she knew better, being as I was so young. I was angry with the people, the people that had failed to protect me, like my father.

I give thanks that as a result of this I, myself didn't become a predator as well. God is good and has blessed me in so many ways and continues to watch over me. I am so glad also that I didn't withdraw myself from society or socially as some do, but I did develop trust issues. Still today I find it troubling trusting people after being let down by so many people before that I had trusted. At this point I would not even give people a chance. My school performance had greatly dropped at one point. I was able to focus and pull myself together in order to succeed and get past this troubling time.

My self-esteem is pretty great considering, but sometimes I don't feel loved by the very people that should be more than willing to love me. I have worked so hard to get where I am on my own. So depending on others is difficult, especially when nearly all the people in my life have been everything but reliable. I have sense met a person however, that has been there through thick and thin and who is unconditional, but this person is to be revealed at a later date and in part two of my life. I can only say that without this person, my journey would not be on track and where it is today and I count my blessings everyday never taking for granted the gift from God that I have been given, and in so many ways.

I felt as though I was missing the key component of being needed by a family unit. I have always wanted to be wanted by others and part of a family. Because I never experienced this, I felt I would go after my own and develop this part of my life. If I would have withdrawn myself from all social aspects of life I would have never been able to move on in life.

My innocence was gone. Lost forever at such a young age. Yet I don't believe that this lady ever quite understood the damage that had been done, nor did she seem to care. Which made the hurt that much deeper. I think due to my abandonment issues with no one ever staying in my life that I have never been able to experience true unconditional love. I have never been able to have that trust when it comes to others. One day I will be able to find this type of love and will cherish it for my life time.

Here we go again

THEN ONE DAY MY ENTIRE world changed all over again. Whether it was based on guilt or pressure from his family, my father took it upon himself to reappear in my life. It is quite possible that he struggled knowing I was out there and not present in his life.

All I could remember was that one day my father pulled up at my stepfather's home, where I was living at the time. It was apparent that his intentions were to relocate me back to Lekki town, the city where his family was residing. This was all happening after I had already completed six years of elementary school. My never-ending pursuit of getting an education continued to face obstacle after obstacle.

I was in the kitchen helping my mother prepare garri, which is a special Nigerian delicacy. It is made from cassava that we had harvested from the farm earlier that evening. As I was getting the meal all set up for dinner, two of my buddies came running towards me, before I could say anything, I could tell from the expressions on their faces that something big was happening.

In unison, they both shouted loudly that my papa was here to see me, I was very surprised, very, very surprised, and a bit nervous. I hadn't seen my father in years. I couldn't quite believe it. I was angered by my friends because I was finding it impossible to believe them. I thought they were playing a cruel joke on me. I went back to getting things ready for dinner. It was then that my mother went outside to see what all the commotion was about.

She returned to the backyard where I presently was with a tall bearded dark skinned man. I could instantly see his resemblance; I could feel the connection too. I could feel that he was my father, even after not being around him for so many years. It was almost like magnetism there. You must remember that this was the first time I had seen my father since practically my birth. That was back when my parents had divorced and went their separate ways.

I was surprised because I never knew him. That day when he arrived I was already 12 years old. He stayed around for a day visit and brought along four of my cousins. We had a cookout, and before they left all four cousins of mine gave me a gift. They got in the car and left. I did not see him again until I was 16. He then took me to live with him.

My mother turned to me and simply said to me that my father was here. I reacted with attitude. Saying things like, who is my father, and that I didn't have one. The man standing in front of me claiming to be my father stopped my moment of denial as soon as I heard his deep voice. Again, I was not sure how to accept him as he was absent for most of my life and I was now a teenager who was almost a man.

My father told me that I was his son and that he was taking me home. Those were the words that came from his mouth. I didn't really like that he seemed to be commanding me. I felt that after everything that I had already been through that I was already grown. What did I need a father for now at this point in my life? Especially since I apparently wasn't good enough for him all this time. I was truly wondering what had changed. Was it a ploy to lure me into some kind of slavery that I had experienced for so much of my life where others would use me to work with no appreciation or compensation? In my mind it was time for me to think about me and to move forward with my own ideas and thrive to do for me.

By now I was angry. So very angry. Angry at my mother and angry at this man in front of me who was saying he was my father. I was ready to attack, yet all I could do was remain motionless. After a moment my stepfather came and ushered my father and I into his living room. By now all the elders and my mother's friends had gathered to see what was going on. My father, whom had been absent all these years, was being welcomed by all that were there. They all seemed so very pleased to see him.

It was then that my father brought out a drink from his bag and offered it to the elders in appreciation for taking care of me over the years. It was a custom. It was at that moment that I thought to myself that I should be getting the appreciation for taking care of myself all these years, because I knew that is what had really happened.

They all continued to listen to my father as he continued to lay emphasis on how he had to come to take me to the city to live with him and his wife and my nine half siblings. I didn't feel right. My gut feeling was one that was making me very nervous. I wasn't sure what to expect. At the same time I did not want to leave my mother, after all she had done for me. I loved her very much. I did not want to leave her as she was the only person that showed me some compassion for a very long time since my grandmother passed.

It was decided that I go with my father to live in their home in the city. I felt that they didn't even take into consider how I might be feeling or to ask me what I wanted, where I wanted to go. If I could have had my own choice, I would have stayed with my mother. I would have completed my high school and then went on to college without any interruption. I very much needed stability in my life. I was not into this at all. I did not want to have change again in my life. I was feeling so very aggravated, mad, hurt, scared, and it was as though it was a bad dream and I just wanted to wake up…Not again…please not again… is all I could think of.

The day I left my mother was crying, all of the emotion was just too much for her to bear. I thought that I would never be able to see her again. It took me a bit, but after awhile, I was excited in a way that this new opportunity had presented itself. Little did I know what I was going to get myself into. Time would tell.

Your life is a result of your own choices. A good life is a result of your own choices. A good life comes about from living for a reason. I had both reason and purpose to live my own life and to make my own choices. Unfortunately I was never given that opportunity. I was simply moved from place to place at others' convenience. Never truly wanted by anyone.

Chasing a dream

IT WAS AGREED UPON BY my parents that my father would put me through high school once I was settled in at his home, my new home. However, it was soon found out by me that my father had no intentions of keeping up on his end of the agreement. It was all a ploy to use me for his on purpose and not thinking about my well being.

While in Lekki town, I was told one morning that school was not an option for me. I was told that I was not school material. I was told that the only option I did have at that moment was to learn a trade. I already knew that an education was the only way to a better life. Otherwise, I would always remain at the mercy of others. I tried to voice my concern but was all too quickly shot down by my stepmother. My life was about to take a turn for the worst.

Then those two, my father and stepmother changed the entire plan. The next day, my father told me to get ready and that I was going to meet someone that will teach me a trade as a rewinding electrician. I was bitter. I wanted to attend school, not learn a trade. Being 16 and a person who felt rebellion from all angles, it was hard to bite my tongue. I obliged to avoid getting into more trouble. In private I would cry when I knew no one was around. I didn't want anyone to know what I was really feeling inside. I was terribly alone. I felt as though my world was so isolated and I was not able to express my feeling to anyone being along as I was. I prayed to GOD for deliverance and to protect me from harm, as I knew he had a bigger purpose for me.

Inside I hated being me. I hated myself for being alive. I constantly would question what I had done to deserve this awful life that I was living. I was at an extreme low point in life. I did not want to go on. What was my purpose why was I here, why did GOD give me life, what was the real reason for my existence and was he going to use me in a different way for bigger and better things when I became a man. Little did I know that my thought was spot on.

There were many days at this time in my life that I had considered not continuing on. I thought about jumping from a coconut tree and falling to my death. I thought about jumping from a moving tractor. There was one that was going to a farm every day and you could actually catch a ride with the tractor. While riding on the tractor is when the idea came to me, but I never followed through. At one point I wanted to drink acid from my uncle's car. The entire reasoning in my mind to end it all was that I would no longer be a problem to anyone ever again. It seemed to make more sense than continuing this every day nightmare. In my mind death was easier than living. Again, GOD is as powerful as he delivered me from the thought of death, as he knew that I was to go on and serve him in much bigger ways and allowed me to hold on through no process of my own. He would deliver me from all that would harm me in time. I now look back knowing that it was a testament of his will and that it formed the foundation for who I would become later.

At that time I did not know what I have, but have since come to realize. Which is that everything happens for a reason. The one thing I did know and that I kept reminding myself of was that I would still have a chance to pursue my dream. My destiny would still be mine. That I only had to believe in GOD to pull me to where I needed to be.

My dream was and always had been to become educated. To become very educated and be successful in life. That's all I wanted everyday all along. When I didn't have proper clothing to attend school, when the kids laughed at me and mistreated me, when I was told I wasn't school material. All this made me want to become educated even more.

When I started the apprenticeship to learn my trade as a rewinding electrician I wasn't going to be getting paid. There was no salary or wages to earn in an apprenticeship. In Nigeria you are not paid while learning a trade during the first four years. You are to depend on your family to survive. That or figure a way to survive on your own. This would include meals, transportation, clothing, etc. for those four years.

In my situation my father would leave my stepmother money for me before leaving for offshore work. But my stepmother would often not give it to me, she would let me go to work without food. Daily I would starve due to her greed. Some of my co- apprentice would offer me portions of their lunches when I was lucky. At the time I was very skinny and unhealthy in appearance.

My stepmother would purchase one set of clothing for me for the season. I was to wear these everywhere and then wash them in the evening when I returned from work. I would then let them air-dry overnight. I would then use a wrapper to wrap them for the night, each day I would repeat these tasks to ensure that I had clothing to wear the next day.

Because my stepmother disliked me so greatly she would deny me as much as she could. She would make it her day's intention to ruin my spirit. She would ask me why I was even there. This hurt me badly. It hurt my feelings, it hurt my pride and it hurt my self-esteem. I was living in agony, in hunger, through abuse, and neglect. I continued to pray that GOD would sustain me through this nightmare and hell.

The will to survive

FELT LIKE IF THERE WAS a hell, that this was it. My stepmother made my life a living hell. I wanted the earth to open up and swallow me. I was kept isolated from my siblings because they were so mean to me. I felt as though I was breaking down, could I go on, was there a purpose for this hell, can I handle the torment, the mental anguish, the frustration, the abuse.

It was my choice to be separated from my brothers and sisters. The things they did to me and ways that they hurt me will forever stay with me both mentally and emotionally. I was the unwanted child and that was brutally clear. I was the child that was forced to do all of the jobs. The child, which was denied meals. The child, which worked beyond fatigue doing farm chores. I was the child that was abandoned and left to cry in this lonely place. I was all by myself. No one there to listen to me. No one there to nurture me. No one there to love me. I was as alone as you could ever be, as a child that just wanted someone to tell me that it was going to be alright. In my mind would I ever be able to function as a normal person – not having the appropriate nurturing or the ability to express myself? Would GOD grant me the common sense to allow me to know right from wrong? Would I ever forgive those who abused me all my life? Would I grow up to be bitter and hateful as they were? I would pray for deliverance on a daily basis and try and stay positive to allow me sanity. GOD takes me from this cruel world of hate and destruction. Hear my prayer is what I would repeat everyday of my life. Why me? Why was it all so divesting? Was this really what they called life?

Nothing I could do would ever please them. They would call me awful names, pick on me and make me feel absolutely worthless. I became conditioned to it and taught myself to live with it. My stepmother would look at me as if I were an alien. Again, I could only pray to help me and to ask GOD to help them. Little did I know that this dysfunction at the time that I was living, also became a positive reinforcement in my life, as I would naturally become compassionate, kind, loving, spiritually fulfilled and love life. At the time however, this view was nowhere in sight. Again, GOD's plan for my future.

Whatever, her mood was that day would be the deciding factor as to which insults she would throw at me that day. I would eat alone. Alone and all by myself at a time when family was thought to be most important. So I would eat alone, because no one wanted me around them. Not being wanted only motivated me to work harder to get out of there. I to this day am a loner, and it is most likely because of that fact.

My hygiene didn't seem to be a priority. I wasn't allowed to take a bath while everyone was still up and awake. There was only a certain time when I was able to clean up, and that was only once everyone was in bed for the night.

Everywhere I went, everywhere I was, it seemed as though there was never room for me. In this case all of my siblings had bedrooms, except me. I used to sleep in the living room every night. It wasn't a big deal. At this time there was no love to be had. The only thing that I could see was this hate that was being thrust upon me. People were not showing me any love. I didn't really mind at this time, as I was not use to receiving love, but was conditioned to giving it. It was all I really knew. Little did I know this would become a survival for future years of my life.

My siblings were all in school, spoon-fed too as truancy was their daily report from school. They engaged in a lot of unbecoming behavior, but my stepmother would cover for them and bribe the police to look the other way. A lot of things also came up missing in the household, and I was wrongly accused of stealing, and duly punished. Those unfair accusations and unwarranted punishments hurt so much back then, and even with the amount of time that has since passed it still hurts, and I will never forget it. I could not figure out how someone like me, who dreamed only of going to school was unable to, not allowed to, yet my siblings who were allowed did not appreciate the gifts they were being given. The gift of education. I later would take my education to the extreme and be a Master Degreed scholar.

Negative behaviors were becoming the daily normalcy. I was continually treated as an outsider and they continued to intercept any money that my father had left for me. I hated how I was treated. At home my siblings would eat, have clean clothing, shoes and a ride to school. I on the other hand would have to walk 10-15 miles to work every morning to my trade job. I was often hungry and not able to sleep well during the night as I had no accommodations.

Things that were taken for granted by them were the things that I struggled to receive a fraction of. I was treated as an afterthought. An object, that just happened to be there. Disrespected, walked on and not made to matter in the least.

I often questioned why I wasn't allowed to go to school. My stepmother decided that I was not school material and that her children were smarter than I was. I was not allowed to read or do anything regarded as educational. I was made to follow a routine. I was to wake, sweep, clean and mop. Then I was to get the water ready for everyone to take a bath. Then clean the car and then get ready for my work.

In the evening I would return to help prepare dinner and serve. Then I would go and sit in my corner. I had a spot that I would sit in until everyone went to bed. Before I could sleep in mine, since it was in the living room I would just wait. Waiting over in my spot. Whenever they had a party I did not sleep at night. They would entertain their guests all night, leaving me unable to go to sleep in the living room where they all were. I wouldn't be able to get any rest. The next day I would struggle at work due to being sleep deprived. No one cared about my well being or gave me any consideration as to my fate. It was expected of me to perform and this is what I did.

There was a day that my stepmother wanted to test my intelligence. She offered me a magazine to read aloud. I was very nervous due to not being allowed to normally read. I started very slowly, then she grabbed the magazine from me and proceeded to tell me how dumb I was and that I was stupid. This was her reasoning as to why I was not allowed to attend school. She was glad she made the decision for me not to go. It was at that moment that I realized that all of my suspicions were correct and that it was her keeping me from getting formal education. It would soon be found that this behavior from her created a desire in me to be an overachiever and accomplish later all that I set out to do.

She continued to degrade me in front of my siblings. Telling them that I wasn't smart enough for school. I was so angry. I was angry and I blamed God for letting me live this way. My siblings would treat me as a slave. At times I wondered if they knew I was their brother based on how they treated me. I wouldn't have been surprised if their mother didn't tell them just that. That I was a slave or just house help.

We didn't have much of a relationship other than the fact that we lived under one roof. My siblings wouldn't normally even speak to me. Unless they needed me to do something such as a house chores or run an errand for them. Even now we do not have a good relationship. They have tried to come back to me and tried to form a close relationship now that they need me, but the hurt they have caused is deep and not the type to repair too quickly. I would say that if this never happens, it will not be something that I regret as these choices were theirs when they were growing up and they chose to treat me with the utmost disrespect and hate. I can only ask GOD to have mercy on their souls as they created this confusion through no fault of my own. I have sense surrounded myself with caring qualified people and do not plan to have my growth interrupted by those who are heartlessness.

I am the child that survived the adversity, and who is still struggling, but standing today. I will make my way as I have chosen this path and I will succeed. As they say what doesn't kill you, makes you stronger. But in my world what doesn't kill you could keep you weary if you don't have the right support system. I did not have any support growing up, but today I am fortunate to have that kind of support. All those years I completely relied on myself, because no one ever was there with what would actually be best for me growing up. They all had their own reasons and motives for trying to help me, which always turned out that it was truly for their benefit only. As I stated, I now have a support system and those in my circle are qualified and true warriors for my cause. I trust them with my life and with them, I will not fail as failure is not an option.

Making it through

IF I THOUGHT THINGS COULDN'T become worse, I was surely wrong. My learning of a trade had ceased due to my father's retirement. When he left his place of employment he decided to relocate the family and start a family business. I wasn't aware that they already had a plan for me. Both my father and stepmother had this great idea to open a cassava processing factory in his home town of Soweto. That is when I was told that I would stop learning my trade to become the machine operator. I agreed and a month later we all moved in order to begin the new business.

At this time my brothers and sisters ranged in age from between the ages of 2 - 19 years old. I was 14 when my father retired and we moved. My siblings were all enrolled into school while I became a cassava processing machine operator for the next two years. I was disappointed and only felt further removed from my dream of going to school. Further from ever making something of myself. Further from ever being successful. And being that it was tradition to just follow along with what was already planned for you, it was doubtful that I would break through and be able to go on my own and follow my dreams.

I tended to believe that I ended up in that circumstance due to not directly having control of the situation. Control was far from what I had. I truly didn't have the ability at that time to do anything other than to follow their orders. It seemed as though this was all a result in my being born out of wedlock. The perception is always different for those born out of marriage. You are there, but you don't really count. You are just a body. Tradition is that you listen to your elders and do whatever it is that they ask of you.

At this time my stepmother was responsible for what I did and when. I began developing resilience to everything. It was in my mind that I could withstand further adversity this way. I realized that I needed to stay motivated and work towards my goals, rather than away from them. All my daily routines were monotonous. I did what I did, because that was what was expected of me. My family depended on me to do so as a form of income. I was a slave to my own family.

I hated that moment of my life. That moment where I realized that I was not a family member. I was being used by my family for my work. All the while I was also being mentally and emotionally abused by my stepmother. I was still made to go to the farm every Saturday to maintain the crops and do the weeding. While at home my siblings were left to sleep in. I knew better than to question the situation.

One day, a sibling cursed at me for challenging her on why a goat was able to eat my food while I was working at the factory. She started crying, told her mother and I got a slap for it. I was then scolded and told to never talk to her dear angel that way again. Everything always managed to happen while my father was not home. And I dared not tell my father or there would be war at home.

I didn't dare tell my stepmother, as she would just find a way to make it my fault. The same would go for if I had told my dad. He wouldn't have believed me, and if he left she would make my life hell so I kept it to myself and just went hungry that day. I was just too small for anyone to take me seriously.

The fury within

THEN ONE DAY THE THOUGHT of not being in school just engulfed me. I was so angry that I stopped working and demanded that I be enrolled into school or else I would no longer work for them. They thought I was bluffing, and didn't take me seriously. I kept up on my refusal to work. Before you know it they were losing money. Yet they continued to deny me my schooling.

This continued for three months. I was striking in an effort for them to see the misery that they were causing me. By the end of the third month, it was me that needed to go back to my routine of working. I felt it was all I knew at this point. It was part of my psychological needs, such as food, shelter and things of that nature.

I took all the money I had collected and boarded a bus to see my mother. I decided that I needed to tell her of the abuse I was suffering.

My mother wasn't surprised. She knew what my stepmother was capable of. The next day my father and stepmother arrived. My mother looked as though she wanted to skin them alive. They lied and said that I was being defiant. They also said that I had stolen money and that I must return home with them. They once again promised to enroll me into high school.

I did steal money to make it home to my mother. My mother knew this, she was a smart woman, and easily figured things out herself. She knew it was not to do something awful, but more as a means of survival. She knew that I had to get out of there. She was so excited to see me. I could tell from looking at her. And that made my heart so happy inside. Everyone in town celebrated it as a homecoming for me. However I was sent back on empty promises once again.

Determined to succeed

ONCE AGAIN I WAS ANGRY. It was even more to my disappointment when I realized that the only reason that they came to retrieve me was because no one wanted to operate the cassava processing machine. As well as they could not afford to hire someone.

Since none of my siblings knew how to operate the machine, and if they did hire someone they would have to pay a salary. Hence I was the only option. This gave me leverage. The leverage that I so desperately needed. With that they finally agreed and enrolled me into high school.

The agreement was to be that I would continue working in the factory every day after school and continue to assist with the family business. I thankfully agreed with the hopes that they would keep up on their end. Knowing that they had already let me down so many times before already in my short life time.

The first day of school was extremely difficult. By now I was already 17 and had missed so many years of schooling. There was so much of a gap in what I had learned and what I was supposed to have learned by now that I couldn't even figure a way of making it all up. No one knew me and they were all sizing me up. I actually had to fight someone the first day, and that was how you gained respect around there.

Not long after I was enrolled into school, I found out that my tuition was not being paid. I was then kicked out of school. When I returned home that evening, I took the money that I had made from the operation and disappointment. Back to my mother I went. It always seemed that in times of trouble I always would find my way back to her. This time was different. My mother spoke to my aunt of my situation. Now my aunt is a no nonsense woman. She told my mom to go home and get some money. So my mother took out a loan from her credit union with the condition to pay back.

The next day my aunt, mother and I traveled to Soweto, where my father lived. That place was the equivalent of a war that day. My father and stepmother were in shock. They went straight to the school and spoke with the principal. My outstanding tuition fee was paid off. But not by my father that had agreed to send me to school countless times, but by my mother.

After that I was transferred to a different school that was near my mother. The new school was very welcoming that my mother had enrolled me in. I did have a problem due to not knowing the language that was being used. They were speaking a tribal language that was different from the one that I was speaking. It was also an adjustment being in a new environment. I realized that my mother had always loved me my entire life. She came to my rescue and lifted my spirits at a time where I was low. I had been knocked down already so many times before.

I still didn't mentally know if I could make it. My goal was to stay in school. I knew that if I stayed in school then there would be hope. I was still being mocked and tormented by some of my classmates due to me being older than the rest of the students due to all of the delays in schooling that I had experienced. I tried my best to deal with my anger issues, I was just trying to be accepted. I just wanted to feel like I was normal. A normal student just going to school like the rest of the students. Instead I was the boy that always wanted to go to school, and never was able to. When finally allowed I didn't know how to really be a student. I had to teach myself what was expected of me and how to succeed.

It was then that I began developing a great mindset. I devoted all of my time and energy to bettering myself, with the help of my mother. I made a deal with her that I would behave, help with the chores, and get a part time job in order to help pay my school tuition.

I rented an apartment near my school which was around 50 miles from where my mother lived. After school I would go out to my folks to work on the farm. They would pay me to work and I could then use that money for rent and tuition. I was planting potatoes as well as other crops, weeding and taking care of the crops so that they would grow strong and healthy. All this seemed worth it for the opportunity to finally be attending school.

Plagued by being busy

MOST CHILDREN HAVE A HARD enough time just being good students without having any other distractions. I was not only going to school as I was also helping my mother with her food business, doing chores at my stepfather's farm as well as taking on a job working at a rubber plantation.

I rented from the owner at the rubber plantation. I would go out and mark the trees that were old enough to produce latex. I would then attend to them every morning before I left for school. Sometimes I would wake as early as 3 am, so that I would be able to collect all the rubber latex from the 800 trees before getting to class. I would do all this and pay rent to the local owner at the end of the month, any money that was left over after that would be put into a savings for my high school tuition fees. I continued with all of these jobs throughout my school years.

I would go out and identify the trees that were old enough to produce. Harvesting latex is much like removing the sugar syrup from maple trees. I would take a juice can and attach it to the tree. Above it I would use a modified knife to cut into the skin of the rubber tree plant. When you penetrate the skin the latex comes out into the can. Then I would go around the next day and collect the juice that had accumulated in the cans. It would take me at least six hours daily to get all of my work there finished for the day.

I was determined that my life was going to be better than that of the one which was handed to me. I continued in school at the time when my peers were settling into hard working jobs that they would stay stagnant in and never move forward. That was not going to be the life for me.

My mother had gone to school and went on to nursing school, where she then found out that she was expecting a child. She then stopped her schooling to become a mother. My father had a high school diploma and went on to hold a prominent position with one of the oil companies. I knew that schooling was a way out. I wanted to go much further than those in my family had before me.

Upon completing high school I decided to move to Lekki town. It is there that all eight of my first cousins lived. The oldest was twenty years my senior and already established. Surely I figured that they would be able to help me move forward.

These cousins were a result of my maternal aunt's family. She gave birth to eight sons that were all educated and successful. Unlike my mother and her children whom struggled every day to make ends meet. This is because my mother allowed a man and her very own family to manipulate her destiny. It was then that I realized that I was responsible for the wellbeing of my own future.

Friends forever

IN SCHOOL I HAD A friend named Emmanuel Edo. We had met through being in the same class. I would tell him all about my problems and any drama that was or had happened in my life. He is a good friend and we have remained friends still until this day. He was there for me to confide in through a rough patch of my life. I never had anyone that would listen to all that had gone wrong in my life and still want to stick around.

Emmanuel lost his mother when he was just two years old, and I didn't know that much about her except through the stories that he had told me. His father remarried and his stepmother owned a local restaurant near school. She used to cook and invite me and Emmanuel to come and eat. I was so lucky to have met Emmanuel and to call him my friend. We would go and play soccer, run around, swim in the river and we would dance traditional tribal dances. We were really good, and we had plenty of fun. I finally felt like a normal kid, growing into a young man.

The town where my school was located, was governed by a monarchy system. One day the monarch's daughter was punished for being a truant. She went home and told her father. He gave the orders to the police to arrest every senior student in my school. Emmanuel was arrested as well as many others. I ran so fast to a nearby bush and escaped being arrested.

The next day the students not arrested rioted. They went straight to the police station.

They broke into the cell houses to retrieve Emmanuel and the other students. It was a very crazy moment. Emmanuel and I used to do lots of things together. We would eat mango from the mango trees after school. We were just teenagers trying to have fun. Those were the days, where I could enjoy my friends. I should have been having those days all along.

At this time I had a girlfriend and her name was Kate Ojo. She was a beautiful girl, very caring, thoughtful and kind. She always smelled of flowers. Her uncle was a very rich man at this time. I never met her father but her mother was always really nice to me. We were together up until I finished my high school. She used to assist me financially since money wasn't a problem for her because she lived a privileged life, whereas I did not. She would always make sure that I had grocery money since that was something I always seemed to be lacking of. She also helped me with transportation and helped to make sure that I got where I was going.

After high school, we both ended up going to the same college. We stayed together the first year and parted when it was time for me to move onto my second school. I had passed my exam and was heading into a new college. I was on my way to becoming successful. I was beginning to get closer and closer to achieving my dream.

Slave to my own family

FINANCES WERE ALWAYS TOUGH. AS time went on I managed to contact my uncle that was already established with his own family and doing well. I struck up a deal with him and his wife in exchange for a place to stay. The deal was that I would come home to his home during breaks from my schooling and weekends and work maintaining the household. This was also to earn money for my school fees.

Initially when I moved to the city and approached my uncle he was not interested in me staying there. A man whom my mother knew had a one bedroom room that he let me use. It was the equivalent to low grade storage in the United States. The accommodations were very challenging. My aunt and uncle seemed very cold when I had met with them that I figure there was no chance of it working out. However about a month later my aunt came and found me. She asked me to work at their home doing the laundry, babysitting, cooking, cleaning and running errands. I agreed to with hopes that this would be a great change from that one bedroom disaster I was currently residing at.

As it began my duties after waking up were to first keep both their cars clean. Next was to wake up their two daughters and get them ready for school and then drive them there. Then I would return back to the house to sweep, clean and make the beds. I was also responsible for having breakfast ready for both my aunt and uncle. I still remember it well. My uncle would have a scrambled egg and tea and my aunt would have hot chocolate. I would also do the ironing, polish shoes and make sure everything was functioning well throughout the family.

After the morning chores were complete I would go to my uncle's office to help run errands until the school day ended. In which case then I would need to go and pick up my nieces. Upon retrieval of the girls, I would return to the office to help my uncle finish up for the day. You would think that this type of work would exhaust me, and that I would need a break. But I never did. I would continue working on and getting things done.

Once I arrived home for the evening I would continue with a different set of chores. Dinner would have to be made, my nieces would have to be bathed and cleaned up and then they would need to be put to bed. While I worked, my uncle would usually stay up and read the newspaper. He would catch up on current events and sometimes he would just stay up late. I would stay awake as well in case he needed something from me. Otherwise, just as I would fall asleep, I would be awakened to do a task for him.

It was difficult but I persevered. I viewed my hardship as a Godsend that inspired me to the highest level of accomplishment. I focused my energy on cultivating only the traits that I needed to be successful. Had I have lacked the hardships, I wouldn't have strived so diligently. I would have settled like all those around me and never looked further.

I applied myself and used the right approach that I had learned to improve myself. With this I was able to accomplish anything and overcome everything that came my way.

At the end of each school break my uncle would offer me my tuition. Only after I would be trying to figure out the costs of my food, clothing and transportation and health care costs would the topic even come up. I began hanging out with friends that were more fortunate than I and it actually worked out well. Those friends were helping me with food and other needs. My friends were helping me to survive, when my family neglected to do so.

I will make it through

IMANAGED TO TAKE ENOUGH EVENING classes that at night I was able to earn my GED diploma. My Aunt would interrogate customers regarding the prices that they were paying to me and the money exchanged to be sure that I wasn't cheating her out of any funds coming into the laundry.

At night I would pack dirty clothes on top of me to keep from being bitten by the mosquitoes. I would still manage to wake up covered in bloody bites. The laundry had no screens due to it just being an unfinished warehouse. It was a swamp like atmosphere, which was perfect for the mosquitoes to infest as a home. Every day I was so very swollen from the bites, and so was the other boy working with me. He managed to develop a fever around the same time I did.

I told my Aunt that I was sick and that I was unable to get up. No matter how hard I tried, I just couldn't get onto my feet. I had all the classic symptoms of malaria; high fever, and shivering were just the beginning. She thought I was lying and just being lazy. She then left me there on the floor and told me to get back to work.

I took it upon myself, and used the money I had made while working at the laundry to buy three tickets for the bus to Ikeja town. There lived my other uncle's wife, who was a nurse. It was a long ride but five hours later we arrived. I had two friends follow along with me to get me on and off of the bus as I was too weak to even stand. Then I paid for their trips back home on the bus. I appreciated their help because I would have never made it to my aunt to receive the help I needed, if they hadn't assisted me in getting there.

Once there my other Aunt gave me an injection to kill the infection. The side effects are itching, and sweating in order to get the poisons out of your body. They gave me food and sent me back to recover. Once back my Aunt at the laundry wouldn't let me return because I had left without permission. This woman left me to fend for myself and now was mad that I had received medical attention when I needed it, instead of working the laundry when I couldn't even stand. I stayed anyways and continued to work at the laundry. I had nowhere else to go. At the time I was working in the laundry, I was also sleeping there. I was still always hungry, as I had been for what seemed like my entire life. So I and an employee that was also sleeping at the laundry, stole a banana and a chicken from the neighbor in desperation. We then killed the chicken and ate it. The boy was underpaid and hungry, and we had to eat. We were losing weight and were well malnourished. After we finished eating we went and confessed to the neighbor. We told him the truth and he forgave us, understanding that we were truly hungry.

My Aunt was so upset over the incident that she moved me into the main house. Where I went to sleeping on the floor in the living room. I was allowed to eat all of my meals except breakfast there. One day I took a piece of bread from the kitchen. My Aunt found out and beat me because she was hoarding food for herself. She then warned me never to touch that bread again. I became accustomed to not eating as much as a growing male should, be in order to be healthy. What you were given was suppose to last, and asking for more would not show strength.

Sometimes she was nice to me, other times she was ever so cold hearted. She was however always very strict. I was thankful that she gave me a place to stay when everyone else rejected me. The business idea was to have me run the laundry. My Aunt met with me once while I was out with my friends and told me to come with her. Then she told me her plans. That included taking me in.

My uncle was very upset that she offered a place for me to stay in exchange for me running the business. I had to stay at the laundry to begin with because he was so angry that she had made a decision without him.

I would spend every day hand washing clothes. It was awful on my skin. It would break open, my fingernails would even fall off. I had such strong determination during the day but would cry at night. It was all I could do to continue to put on a strong face and carry on. In hopes that all of this hard work would one day pay off.

My Aunt had later left to go to the United States due to a high risk pregnancy she was in the midst of. She left behind her husband and two children at the time. They were ages 3 and 2. Back then she left them, with no intentions of returning back to her family in Nigeria. I helped to raise the children and have maintained a solid relationship with them throughout the years. The situation between her and my uncle had grown into a chaotic relationship over the years. If I had been in my aunt's shoes, I would have done the same by leaving and never coming back. After all I already took care of the children here, and she knew she could trust me in continuing to do so.

Her reason for leaving was that the new baby was going to need treatment that was unavailable here at home. They have since divorced and she has now remarried and created an entirely new life. I continued to stay with my uncle until I finished college and helped to raise the children. She managed to keep in touch with me, but since I got married she decided to separate herself once again.

Never enough time

TIME IS WHAT SOME SAY is the most precious element of human existence. During my school days, the only person I didn't have time for was myself. My schedule was so busy that I kept myself focused. I wanted to be able to do fun stuff while in college, but thankfully it was my lack of free time which ended up keeping me out of handcuffs.

I began exercising every morning for at least thirty minutes to keep my energy level up so that I could focus in class. This was the only way I could cope with my terrible hardship that I was experiencing at that time. Exercising built my energy level up and helped reduce my fatigue. Being in great physical condition helped me to deal with my issues of stress and depression. It would also enable me to deal with any challenges I encountered in my journey.

I made my own dumbbells out of concrete and a pole. It wasn't appropriately measured to be even, but it worked and I curled my ass off. It was in my mind that if I needed something that I would have to furnish it on my own. Working out was my therapy, and it still continues to be even today. I think that if I hadn't begun working out that I would have gone crazy.

I stayed extremely busy, doing things which my then circumstances, permitted me to do. Instead of doing the things that I would have preferred to do with my life. I wouldn't allow adversity to stand in my way. I couldn't afford to fail a class and to drop out of school. If that would have occurred, I would have kissed my opportunity to earn a degree goodbye.

I only learned to improve myself through not giving in to being too tired or not having enough time. If I were to succumb and begin feeling bad for myself now, I would have had a serious problem. I was able to avoid letting myself sink, due to my positive outlook that I had developed.

Eating balanced meals was far from what was happening. It was a time where you were just happy to have something in your stomach. If food was fresh you were more likely to be able to get it to eat, I wasn't able to have a garden so I had to rely on grocery stores and the food they had that I was able to afford.

Lack of time and energy could have kept me from completing my education and accomplishing my dream. But I was able to rise above it and continue on. Exercising would also give me energy, an energy that I didn't have before. It gave me hope that one day things would be different.

Falling into something more

DURING MY SECOND YEAR IN college I met my first real girlfriend. I was in the cafeteria at school and stumbled into her. We both exchanged a few words in which she invited me to a Christian gathering. From that moment on we were together. She was amazing. Very intelligent as well as beautiful. She was everything that I had thought that I wanted in a woman. She had long beautiful straight hair, good height, cute face and a real feminine way of walking. She was well organized, and managed to stay alluring while she was also a hard worker. She came from a well to do family and was very generous towards me.

We did almost everything together. We would go to church, travel together, cook together and just enjoy each other's company. We were like two in one as we could barely spend time apart. We were absolutely wonderful. At the time she was everything I needed. She made friends with my mother and siblings and became very close with my family. I told her everything. How I was shipped from family member to family member as a child. How I always seemed to be struggling for the necessities in life. I finally felt like someone cared about me and was doing their best to look out for me.

She was my world. I was very loyal and faithful to her and I thought she was as well. Then one day when I was at her house she voluntarily confessed to me that she had cheated on me with her next door neighbor. She told me that she was in the company of some of her girlfriends that decided to stay the night in one of the dormitories. She fell asleep, and they ended up leaving her. She told me how she felt hands on her body, and how she liked it and then how she did not try to stop what was happening, although she knew it was wrong.

I was heartbroken. I opened myself up only to be hurt. She apologized and we managed to patch things up, but things were never the same from that moment on. I tried to forgive her, I just couldn't bring myself to get past it. I was still in shock that it had even happened. I was never able to trust her after that. We ended up parting ways when I was sent in one direction to serve the government and she was drafted to a different area.

For the first time ever I had cried my eyes out, beyond control. My feelings were so hurt. Before then I was always able to keep my emotions in control. I was deeply affected by this for years to come. I refused to be brought down by this again. I was truly broken.

Becoming friends with the bad guys

JOINING A FRATERNITY WHILE IN college seems like almost a sort of rite of passage. In Nigeria it's different. They have confraternities. Which are more dangerous than you would ever want to believe.

The first pyrites confraternity was created as a social organization for promising students. However as new confraternities were formed, they became increasingly violent. Across the national higher learning institutions of Nigeria through the 70's and 80's an entirely different world was happening on and off campus.

By the 90's most confraternities operated as criminal gangs, called campus cults in Nigeria. Besides normal criminal activities these cults have been linked to political violence, school riots and crisis in Niger Delta of Nigeria.

When I started University at Benin, Benin City, Edo State Nigeria, I was approached by a member of family confraternity, also known at the time as campus mafia. This one came into existence in the 90's, yet today they maintain a presence at numerous schools throughout Nigeria. The man that approached me was very nice and polite to me, his name was Mr. Matthew Grant. Things that made me approachable by him were my looks, my size, my grade in school and my financial status. He took me out for a drink and we spoke for a long duration. When we had finished talking he asked me to join his cult. He said that this fine cult was the only confraternity on campus that could protect me from any danger.

At the time I was in my 20's and wasn't really interested in joining any cult at all based on their reputation and known actions. But you can't just bluntly refuse the offer, or you could face serious consequences. I remember hearing and seeing on the television about students killed from rival cults. There was extreme hooliganism, violence and a bloody struggle for supremacy between rival cults on campus. It brought death to many innocent students. Heads were actually being chopped off in broad daylight on campus between the rival gangs. Name any violence you could imagine and most likely it happened.

I was very mindful of making my decision as to whether to join or not. Nigeria was not peaceful at this time, especially on campus. There was a great deal of fighting. There were rival gangs that would use axes, knives, machetes and guns to kill each other. There would actually be bodies lying around on campus. We would all then go ahead and follow the safety protocol.

Rough and tumble

I RENTED A ROOM ON CAMPUS together with other students to save money. I thought that it was really something great. I had met them on campus and we all needed a place to live. We would go out and look for girls, eat together and just hang out. They were into clubbing, drinking, smoking weed, but they were all really smart. They always made it to class and did well. That was before I realized that the other guys belonged to another cult and were each other's family.

The one guy Patrick, was a womanizer, he thought that he truly was God's gift to all women. He would not cook or clean and of the group he lacked in the brilliance department. He loved soccer and was a huge fan of his favorite soccer team, Arsenal. Then there was Chuck, he was a skinny light skinned boy. He was from the Eastern part of Nigeria. He was the fearless one, he was also very talkative and pretty cocky in his conversations. All he wanted to do all day was to smoke cigarettes. Then there was a female, Ndali. She was very rough. Rough and scared of nothing. She would fight any girl that came her way. She loved going to the clubs, and she loved having sex. She would thrive off of being sexual, as though it were her therapy.

I was very naïve. Always being nice to them. I would sometimes cook and ask them to eat. I often would share my personal items with them just trying to be nice. Before long they took advantage of me and mistook my kindness as a weakness.

They quickly started plotting against me. At one point the rent was due from my end, and I wasn't able to afford it. I promised that I was going to pay but it never came through. I borrowed some money from one of the boys and needed to pay that back as well. I was going to go and visit a lady that I grew up with when I was younger, but then she told me that things had changed and that the money had run out. I had to then try to raise money to get back to the school. I was not only broke but I would be returning with no cash for the rent. When I told them that I did not have the money they ganged up on me. They were furious.

One night when I went out, one of them who claimed to be the headman took the only pair of shoes that I had and decided to keep them for himself. My ex-girlfriend bought those shoes for my birthday and they were my only shoes. They also took my food and hygiene supplies. When I noticed, I was very upset. I was ready to do anything to prove that I was a man just like they thought they were.

I decided to approach them politely to try and have my items returned to me. But they wouldn't go for it. Instead they all started laughing and teasing me. Calling me Jews, which meant that I was weak. When I heard that, I became very sad. I was ready to make a move that I would later come to regret.

I started mentally telling myself to do something to earn their respect. I knew that I had to do something quickly or I needed to get myself to the university authorities and report the incident. The boys kept talking crazy to me. They just wouldn't stop.

Then I lost it. I charged the one boy and picked him up. I hit him hard against the ground and then the rest joined in on the fight. I picked up a heavy object from the floor to defend myself. Three of them ran. I was able to pin one down. I continued to administer punches until he passed out. I was going to end his miserable life. Then I remembered that portion of the bible that clearly said 'thou shall not kill'. When I stopped he got up from the ground and ran, he ran faster than I have ever seen someone run. He went and told his fellow gang members. Which brought only a larger trouble to me. It is one thing if you are in an individual fight. You throw some punches, someone wins, someone loses and you all go home. But once you involve gangs into the mix, then you have a large number of people that all want to fight you. I reported the incident to the school authority but was later told by a reliable source that the investigator was also a member of the cult to which the boys belonged.

A means to stay alive

WHEN I RETURNED TO MY room, I decided to move out as quickly as I could to a different dorm. At this time I knew I would have to do something to protect myself for the rest of my stay on campus or else I wouldn't make it out alive.

I started thinking about joining a cult. It was the only way I would be able to survive. I knew that I had to join after beating my roommate that was a member of one of the notorious confraternities on campus. These folks would kill whether they had a reason or not.

The next morning I went straight to Mr. Grant, the mafia man, who previously had approached me to join. I told him about my experience with my roommates the prior night. I also told him of my interest to be one of the mafia. He looked at me, shook my hand and said congratulations. It was then when I asked for protection. I told him at this point I really needed to join and have the rest of his gang to help protect me as one of their own. I had told him the whole story of what had happened and he agreed to have all of the members look out for me. They took the guy that had taken my belongings, and instigated the fight and brought him out into the bush and beat him badly. That was his punishment for him trying to start a problem between two rival gangs. From that moment on he treated me with respect and he never crossed my path again.

Mr. Grant was very proud of me. We ate, drank and had fun with the girls at the club that we were at that evening. The next day he told me that he would come and get me later that day. He later called and informed me of the initiation ceremony which would last for twelve hours, all night in a forest far away from the city.

I was picked up and managed to pass the test phase where I was asked all sorts of questions. Some of the questions were along the lines of them telling you a secret and then seeing later if you relayed it to anyone else. Among them if I would be willing to kill in order to protect others? I answered that yes, I would do this. Would you be loyal, would you respect the cult? They also wanted to know if you would have enough to eat, were well groomed, as well as if you had a place to live.

We arrived to the initiation venue. I was ordered to step down from the vehicle while blindfolded, along with the other candidates. I can't remember how many of us there were because I was too nervous. I didn't know what to expect.

I asked myself if it was supposed to be a bed of roses, why were we being blind-folded. We were walked into a deep forest, where no one else except the cult members could hear the activities including the police. We were forced to drink a heavily mixed high volume of alcohol. Only God knows what other controlled substances were mixed in with the alcohol. I was drunk immediately. I could barely move. I was weak, I was scared.

Then they started beating the other candidates. I couldn't see them because I was still blindfolded. But I could hear them crying for God's help. We were being beaten by the mafia veterans. And only God knows by how many.

They hit us with thick sticks, rods, machetes and metal objects. The first few hours I was in so much pain that I thought I would die. After so many hours into the abuse I couldn't feel the pain anymore. Everything just stopped. I couldn't feel anything at that point. All I knew was that I was still there. I was still breathing.

People actually did die during the ceremonies. They were abandoned in the forest. I was surprised that I survived the initiation because it wasn't designed to be easy by any means. I most certainly could have died during the initiation and would never have been heard or seen of again. However, it was worth the risk in that if I hadn't joined the other gang would have most definitely tried to kill me. I was a target on campus after the fight and was already identified. They were notorious for killing, raping, anything awful that you can think of, they did.

The next morning I was dropped off by the cult member at a strategic point and we were warned not to tell anyone about the initiation, including the police. It took me over a month to recover from the initiation. Any one that had asked I simply explained to them that I was in a car accident. During that time of recovery I reflected as to whether the process was really necessary. Over the years I was asked to help in the initiation process with others and I always was able to come up with an excuse. Most members would be excited to participate and would want to beat the participants badly. They would want to get even. I never felt this, and would decline participation and would instead leave to go and study for a test or similar, just to get away from it all.

The heist

THERE WAS A TIME WHEN I was to be feared. I was living in a hostel, off campus with the cult. There was always something awful happening, and more times than not we were involved. The guy that was second in command would decide which places and people we would terrorize. We would go on runs and cause chaos around the area. One day it was decided that he had a big deal in the works and was finalizing the plans to make it all go down. This was to be one for the history books.

Normally when they would fight a rival gang, I would take off as far away as I could, when they would start talking of the preparations. All I wanted was to get through school…. Alive. I would leave campus when something was about to go down. People would die, this was the real deal, and I didn't want to be a part of it.

The day before I worked and came back from classes. I was already tired from a long day. I was finally let in on what the big deal actually consisted of.

We were going to rob a bank.

Not just any bank, but the one on campus. It had never been attempted before and we were going to be the ones that would do it. We figured that we would have all that cash and that we would be seen as heroes of some sort.

After all of my years of not being able to afford to eat, I finally had a chance to have access to all that money to be able to feed myself. I admit, that I was excited by all of this, but at the same time scared for my life. Meanwhile something kept telling me that if I went through with this that I was going to die. In Nigeria police shoot on sight. There are no trials, no proving your innocence. It is as simple as that, they see you commit a crime and they kill you, shoot you dead.

The time had come and we all got onto motorcycles to head to the meeting spot to decide each of our roles that we would play in this. Then it happened, the fear, the reality, all of it consumed me. It consumed my entire soul. I just wanted to finish school and graduate I didn't want to be a part of any of this nonsense. My mind began searching for a way to get out of there. A way to stay alive. Then it came to me. I crawled into the nearby bushes, and like that, I disappeared.

They were all so high and fired up that they didn't even seem to notice at the time that I was gone. My plan had worked. I had left the campus for two weeks to stay in Warri. I figured this would allow enough of a cool off period. Then it was time to return to the campus.

I pretended that they had left me in the forest. I reported that I was abandoned, to the overall mob person. I explained my story and it saved me. God helped me that day by giving me the right words to say. People around me were dying on campus and I survived. As if God was helping to make it through safely. I felt as though He had greater plans in life for me.

Fear of an AK47 bullet through my skull scared me. I had never been scared like that before. Something was there in my heart, something was definitely keeping me alive. My one friend Chuck was really involved within the cult. He had absolutely zero guidance in life. No father, no one. He lived each day by trial and error. He would confide in me and told me stories that I still cannot remove from my mind. Times were different then, times were hard. Life continued to be a struggle.

There were monthly dues that had to be paid, and they added up to be quite expensive. If you couldn't afford to pay you would get beat up. There were people and their sole purpose was to hunt for members that didn't pay. They were known as the enforcers. Before you join they speak of nothing of initiation, dues and responsibility. To get out you have to be beaten out. The same way you came in. They would kill you if they had to. The goal was to protect your own. Screw up and you were a dead man.

They managed to rob the bank, but didn't make it out with all the cash they had expected. They continued to be a public nuisance and would get on buses and rob all the people on board. They would harass everyone and force girls to be with them. They tried their best to intimidate the world. The gang is forever lasting. Once you're a part of it you are in it for the rest of your life. The day before graduating a good friend of mine and member of the gang, walked out of his dorm only to be shot in the head and killed. All those years he put into schooling and now he died, the day before we were finished. Once I graduated I served my time in the paramilitary and traveled. I was in federal capital territory. All university graduates must serve 1 year at least or they will be arrested. Upon completion you are given a certificate that you must present for future employment. I worked as a Nigerian Youth Service Officer. There I was drafted to a local school to teach business classes.

Looking for something more

IT IS BY NATURAL INSTINCT to love and feel the need to be loved back in return. In an effort to try and find something new I found myself going online and signing up for one of those dating websites. A friend in a café referred me over to one in particular and I figured that I would give it a try. I placed my best picture and filled my profile with my age, race, height and social activities. I was completely honest with everything that I had written. It never occurred to me to be anything less than truthful. I began by posting positive and inspirational messages when I caught the attention of an American female. We became online friends and talked for quite a while before we started discussing that we should meet.

If one can recall that my entire past was spent trying to please others. Never having anyone that truly had shown genuine interest in me and what I wanted out of life, the woman online and I began messaging each other. It was a wondrous feeling to be on the receiving end of all this attention. She was wonderful, and she promised to come and meet me in Nigeria. Things were finally looking up.

However, my new friend was similar to the stories that you hear regarding websites in which people seem better than they really are. She suggested that I come and move to the States to be with her. At first I declined, because in my culture the female moves in with the male, not the other way around. She was unable to move to Nigeria due to having a teenage daughter that was still in school and she felt would not be able to withstand the summer's heat. I eventually agreed and made the decision to move to America. I truly believed I was in love with her and wanted nothing more than to be with this woman that said she cared so very much for me.

Love is different for everyone. Some say it's that feeling when you can't hardly handle being away from that special someone. Others may say that it is mutual caring that is beyond what any friendship could ever bring. I believe that love is that feeling you get in the pit of your stomach deep down that is so very strong. Stronger than you had ever felt before. You experience this feeling when you are around that certain someone and when you merely think of that person. Deep down you feel that in that moment nothing else could ever matter. Whether it is the attraction, affection, or the simple enjoyment it feels as though it is all of those feelings rolled up into one emotion. It is the greatest feeling in the world.

When you are truly in love you know it. It does help however, if you already have a solid and honest love for yourself. You need to be able to give without asking in return. You can't be judgmental and selfish towards each other. You'll realize that you feel extremely comfortable around this person that you care so much about. Almost to the point of losing all of your inhibitions. Most of all you feel such a strong attachment that you want to be near them as much as possible.

You'll be concerned for their wellbeing. Their feelings, desires and needs will also become your feelings, desires and needs. When you experience all of this, you will then know that you have found true love at last. This was the love I was longing for all of my life, even up until now.

Preparing for the journey

BEFORE COMING OVER TO THE States I did my fair share of research. I wanted to know as much as possible about the land, the people, the culture and how things worked over here. I was amazed that the United States has over 300 million inhabitants. The people seemed able to entertain themselves through the arts, music and theatre. The land aspect was so diverse that I had trouble believing it. There were mountains, lakes, rivers, coastlines and deserts. All this in one country was hard to believe.

I also found it interesting that the United States has a democratic government elected by the people. There are several official symbols of the country such as the Bald Eagle, the White House, the American Flag, the song Star Spangled Banner. Then there are the landmarks. You could easily look at the Lincoln Memorial, U S Capitol, the Liberty Bell, Mount Rushmore, and the Statue of Liberty as a symbol of the United States of America. I also realized through research that the United States encompasses the good and the bad, the crazy and the sane. It is like a giant tapestry that has woven into it the ideas, dreams, and desires of its many diverse cultures and citizens.

Nigeria, as you may imagine, is very different from the United States. It is very ethnically diverse and not separate as much as in the States. It is more intermingled and integrated to a larger extent. However all ethnic groups retain their language and customs and stick to them. This cultural mix has led to confusion on social, political and economic levels. Ethnic conflicts and arguing seem to be a never ending ordeal of the Nigerian social and political landscape. There has been plenty of ethnic conflicts that have been taking more and more of a toll on the development of the entire country. The change has caused bloodshed. Many issues all while working towards gathering more political benefits and economic gains for the group that is concerned within the context of the democratic dispensation. They are still trying to fulfill all of their aspirations.

My lady friend that I was to meet, told me all sorts of wonderful things about how great the states are and the opportunities that are here to be had by all. The idea of opportunity and acceptance seemed like an amazing dream come true to me. There were people from every background imaginable in the states and they all comingled and got along. It was like a fairytale. However, I did not realize that the town I was going to was not a large flourishing city, but instead a small rural town in the state of Indiana. To my demise, the area was not rich with culture, the arts and was certainly not the area for growth.

It also never dawned on me that this overwhelming acceptance of everyone may only be felt in areas of the country and not specifically by all the residents. I never thought that someone would dislike me based on where I came from or the color of my skin.

Finding myself

IT'S AMAZING THAT I MOVED off to another country, another continent all for a chance at love. I moved across an ocean knowing that I would only know one person when I arrived. Away from where I grew up, from my family, from everything I knew. Off to the land of opportunities as they call it. However, and very soon, I would find that the land of opportunities would bring adversity to me as the area was not thriving nor was the ability for the person that I had fallen in love with, strong enough to carry our goals as a couple to a higher level. There was baggage that I was not aware of.

I began a job at the local YMCA a few months after I moved here, as the front desk assistant and soccer coach. It was a way for me to meet people and make new friends. I also started to visit local churches on Sundays and attend bible studies on Friday nights. I was beginning to slowly meet the community a little at a time. I met a friend at one of the nearby parks that told me that I could meet people from all walks of life at the soccer field, which, I in turn did. I am still friends with many of them today. Soccer was a sport that I loved in Nigeria. I was also very good.

Some of the people here were very narrow minded and prejudice was a real factor that I was not expecting to deal with. They did not seem to be aware of anything outside of their own small comfort zones. It has to do with the fact that these rural areas were not diverse and did not rank high in cultural diversity. They had never traveled, never been around folks from different places, and I was not use to people like this. It required additional adapting on my part. These people were very judgmental and I was not prepared to defend myself. It was turning out to be a disaster in the making. However, some of those people opened their minds after realizing that I was not a threatening African, but more a soul that was lost and made his way into their area.

My accent seemed to be troubling for some people, where they had difficulty in understanding me, which caused frustration. I was able to take a class in accent reduction and was able to get a better job where people were able to better understand me. I found that the area was very limited as far as diversity goes, and that it was not the residence fault, but my goal to make an effort for understanding, as that is who I am. I never have an issue taking responsibility and for some, I take their inadequacies, to better myself.

My lady friend was another matter on its own. She was all for me coming to the United States and leaving my whole world behind. However, she turned out to be the type that doesn't think things through before doing them, rather impulsive. I was only 31, while she was six years my senior at 37. Our relationship seemed great before I moved here, but once I set foot on American soil, she became very controlling of me, as if I was her possession. Sometimes she was a really nice person and other times when she forgot to take her medications, she would become unstable and make poor choices. She also was the type that when she promised you something, she would do it 100 percent. The same goes for when she promised to ruin you.

Losing it all again

IN 2005 SHE FILED FOR divorce and kicked me out of our home. I didn't even know what divorce was. We never spoke of anything like that in Nigeria. Family took care of family, regardless of problems. Without warning she placed all of my belongings onto the front porch and told me to leave. I didn't know what to do, where to turn. I was officially homeless. I was not Americanized to cause an issue and took her aggressive demeanor at face value. Thankfully, a friend of mine George, took me in for a couple months to help me get situated. My lady friend withdrew her divorce filing and didn't file again until 2007, at which time she did see that one through. I felt relieved that it was over and the divorce allowed me to move forward with my life. Another friend of mine was able to help me get hired at LaPorte Juvenile Detention Center, where he already had worked. We worked together there for over four years. I was then able to save money and was soon able to get a place at an apartment complex. I finally felt that I was independent and was able to start working to achieve other things for myself without having anyone interfere.

I was able to pick up a job with the Indiana Department of Corrections at their Westville Facility. Not too long after, I took on a second job at the area Juvenile Detention Center. There I worked as a youth social worker assisting troubled kids. I would help them to learn skills that would help them better themselves. I noticed the impact I was having on them. I decided to volunteer my time helping troubled kids in the area complete their community service responsibilities in the community.

The rewards of volunteering are endless. In addition to improving the community and advancing causes that I believed in, I was also developing new skills myself and creating an awareness for others to grow as people themselves. It also raised my own confidence and instilled a pride in me that I was making a difference. I was making new friends as well as making a differences everywhere I went. I loved it.

My ex and I had been talking and I decided to allow her to move into my apartment with me in order to help her get back on her feet.

My ex wife who seemed supportive of me making new friends decided that she really wasn't. She decided to not allow me to have friends, especially female friends. I was trying to help her to get on the right medicines to control her mood swings, but she would hear nothing of it. I was helping her to financially get back on her feet at this time as well, but she never did. Some people cannot be helped.

I was then motivated to put myself back into school and push forward to receiving my Master's degree. I continued to develop my leadership and management skills each and every day. I became even more involved in my community. I majored in Business while in college and have been very successful from doing so.

Around this time, one of my bosses at the correctional facility received a call from her claiming that I only married her to get into this country and that I should be fired. My superior called me in and spoke with me regarding the matter. I had told him and a few others how she still was in love with me and decided that if she couldn't have me then no one could. She also seemed wrapped up in the idea of having me deported.

The boss later wrote a letter in regards to my legal status in the United States that told of the entire situation. He was impressed with not only my work record but even more impressed with how I was continuously trying to better myself. I was working my job there at the facility, the part time job at the juvenile detention center and putting myself through the university to earn a degree. He told me that he would do what he could to support me because I was such a fine employee.

Mind you, I was married in 2003, and gained my citizenship in 2007. It was three to four years of pure torture. I came over here for love, not a green card. Initially I had asked her to relocate to Nigeria too live with me and she refused. She convinced me to come here because she would not be able to survive the heat of Nigeria.

This woman was full of mood swings. She would go from being loving to jealousy and anger. Then she would be right back at loving and to the point of being clingy. I had so much to give, so much ambition inside and she was holding me back and trying to control me every step of the way. A few weeks after my boss received that first call, he received another. This time it was her apologizing for calling him earlier and saying that she was having a hard time with the divorce and that she still loved me.

A number of months later I was summoned back to his office because she was at it again. She decided that she was going to bring the INS into it and try to get me in trouble that way. I had applied for a permanent work visa but still needed an employer sponsor. So it was decided that the Westville Correctional Center would be proud to endorse me. He completed the paperwork and turned it in.

Later I needed to contact him again because I was in need of letters of recommendations from people that knew me and knew my intentions and the struggles of being here. I had a couple of friends, her niece and my former boss write letters to help me in my efforts to make it through this time in my life. I had finally found a life here for myself here, where I could progress without being mentally and emotionally abused and she was going to see to it that it would be nearly impossible for me to enjoy.

The dream survives

IN 2007 THINGS WERE BEGINNING to get better. A friend of mine had offered to host me in London, so I decided to go ahead and visit the United Kingdom. It was September and we went to the Nigerian Independence Day Party in London the night of the 28th. I traveled as often as I was able, during weekends and vacations. I still remember as if it were yesterday. That is where I met my now wife Ekene. I could see that she was very intelligent, kind and well spoken. We had such a good time that evening that we decided to meet the next day for brunch at her place. Which turned out to be a dinner at her mother's flat due to us all being so tired and sleeping through breakfast and lunch.

Her maternal uncle was visiting at the time from Nigeria and I had a very lively discussion with everyone and an instant connection with them all. We spent hours talking in the living room while the females went off to braid hair. It all just felt very natural. Like things finally clicked. After we ate dinner, Ekene was informed by my host that I would be leaving to go back to the states in the morning. She then took it upon herself to drive me to the airport. She didn't have to do that, but it was just her kindness that emits from her and the type person she was at the time.

Before my flight we had breakfast at the airport and before I boarded we exchanged contact information for each other. When I arrived and was safely landed I emailed both my host and Ekene to let them know that I made it home. After that we began exchanging emails quite regularly. We started chatting online whenever we were able to and began developing an amazing friendship. I then asked for her phone number. I was able to call her then and hear her sweet voice again.

Towards the end of October she went to visit her father in Vienna, Austria. While there she heard the awful news that a very good friend of hers had passed away during childbirth. I was the first person that she had called in her time of need. I tried my best to console her and make her feel better. It wasn't too long after that, to make matters worse, I had heard that my cousin had passed away in Nigeria of meningitis while visiting his parents, And my Aunt died from cancer in Nigeria all around the same time. Ekene returned the favor and did her best to make me feel better. She made me feel secure, loved, and needed. All things I was craving but could never find a way to obtain them. May have been again, a false security, as I did not really know how to differentiate real love from that of need.

By the time she had made it back to London we were well on our way to getting to know each other better with each and every day. By December she had decided to make a trip to the United States to be able to visit me on my own turf. There she could see the environment I live in, meet me and generally get to know me at "home" so to speak.

She arrived on the 27th of December, 2008 in Chicago and from there we drove the hour drive back to where I lived in Michigan City. From there we went on a road trip to Toronto, Canada for New Year's Eve and spent five days visiting with my cousins before heading to New York to visit friends. From there, we went to visit family in Georgia and then finally back home.

We spent a total of fourteen days on that visit. We had talked about dating prior to her visit. I had told her that I had been married before and was now divorced, and we talked about the negativity that was involved in my first marriage and how not all marriages are like that. She on the other hand had never been married but had intentions of one day doing so when she met the right guy. Ekene also told me that the end result of any relationship was marriage and that the only way she would agree to dating me was if I were open to the possibility of one day being married again.

I was 35 at this time and getting older. We discussed how we would expand ourselves, do business, add value to ourselves. One thing we did not cover was expectations and boundaries, which I now realize are things that you should talk to your potential life partners about and compromise a basic agreement to prevent future issues.

She said that the way she saw it and still sees it today is that if we both give it our best shot and it doesn't work out, then at least we can say that we really tried. Anything less would be sabotaging the relationship and destroying it before it even has a chance to develop.

She returned back to her home and we continued to talk through phone calls, chatting and video calls. In March she returned again to Indiana to spend time with me for my birthday. She arrived on the 13th and stayed until the 30th. At this time it was safe to say that we were in a relationship and trying our best to make it work despite the distance.

Mapping my future

MY FAMILY WAS LEARY AFTER my divorce from my lady friend, and worried since I was so far geographically from them. They didn't want me to have to face any additional adversities in life. So when I began speaking to my mother about the lovely woman that I had met in London, my mother listened with a touch of protectiveness. They didn't care about race, they just wanted a well-rounded and behaved woman for me.

After Ekene returned back to the United Kingdom, I informed her that my mother would like to speak to her. I had been telling my mother about this wonderful woman and she wanted to have a chance to get to know her as well. Now my mother was still in Nigeria and Ekene was in London, at this time they would call each other as well as my younger sister Patience, whom has since passed away. Due to some personal problems Ekene had to take time off work in April. Her plan was to go and spend time with her father in Vienna, Austria while she recovered and was deciding what she was going to do next and where she would go next.

By now everyone in her family was aware of whom I was and I was accepted by them as being her boyfriend. So off she went to Vienna and returned a month later to London. She felt pretty much the same after a few months and finally decided to resign from her job. At that time she had decided to come spend some time with me over the summer here in the United States. She was here this time from May 15th to July 16th 2008. One day before she left to go back to London I proposed to her and she accepted. She portrayed the exact type of woman that I was looking for.

I had bought a ring and planned the entire evening out. It was romantic and the perfect mood was upon us. We had just come from dinner, when I had walked in the door and picked up the ring and looked directly at her. Straight into her eyes, I spoke and asked her, from the bottom of my heart, to marry me. She shouted out that yes she would and was beyond excited. We both were. We were in love.

We decided to wait until she was back in London before telling our friends and families. I planned to take some time off work to visit my family in Nigeria in November and we agreed it would be a good time to have a formal introduction for both families. As time went by, we began planning for the introduction ceremony. Realizing that the cost of the ceremony in 2008 and the Yoruba traditional engagement later on as well as a church blessing would be financially tasking we decided to go ahead and get married in Nigeria in November of 2008.

We had two weddings. One was a traditional and one was a white wedding. At the traditional one we wore traditional Nigerian dress called agbada. While at the white wedding I wore a suit and Ekene wore a formal white wedding gown. Both events were formal in their own rite. People came from all over Europe, Africa and all over the world to attend our big event. There were over 500 guests in attendance. We held the traditional wedding on Friday, and the white wedding the next day on Saturday. There was music, lots of music including African band music at both.

Things felt so much different this time around. I knew this would be my forever. The reception of everyone went so well. We fit together very well. Everyone gave us a wonderful reception and wished us many years of happiness and joys. We understood each other. We understood our culture, our food, our clothing. We may not have had the same goals but we were off to a great start.

There, began the rest of my life, her life and our lives together with one another to help each other through the good times, the bad times, and all of those in between.

Figuring it all out

A NYONE COULD TELL THAT NO two people are the same. Things that bring me joy may upset another and things that upset me may bring them joy. Well my current support system is not the type to express her emotions over situations. I am sure that she understands all that I have been through to an extent, but she really hasn't ever talked much about it and how she really feels about it, since we have been together. Growing up for me was different than that of the average child here. I had many more barricades to break through and hurdles to get myself over. And the majority of it I did all on my own. I learned not to rely on anyone and that more often than not it is just easier to do things yourself.

I have gone to great detail in an attempt to make her understand my life from the time we began dating until even now. Over the years I have managed to suppress some of the events. Mostly, because they were just too hurtful and traumatic to relive. Still today some of my past still affects me in my everyday life. Maybe it causes me to pause before making a decision, maybe it stops me so that I take a moment to be so ever thankful for where I am now and surviving that place I was before.

And while I do get some support from my union in small areas, she has never fully understood my hearts desire to become the man I have chosen to be. With this being said, I get no support from my partner in this area. It's not something you can force, as this is a choice and not one for me to make for her. I realize that she too has her own life challenging situations to worry about as well. We have a mindset that helps us to maintain ourselves when being challenged in life. My partner is able to lead her own life and free to go after her own dreams, just as I am myself. She enjoys crafting when she has time, as well as making new friends. She enjoys writing and reading.

I was blessed with having a daughter and now a son. I am now a father, and I know that my role is to love, care and prepare my children for their lives one day on their own. I know that we all begin completely dependent on our parents as children, but since I was always lacking one or the other, I figure I might as well be the greatest one I can be. I believe that if I raise my children successfully that they will live as self-respecting and self-responsible adults as they grow up. They will then be able to confidently face and cope with all the different challenges of life.

Of course not all adults are the same. As they grow, the will have differing levels of confidence, optimism, self-esteem and self-worth. Each of these characteristics are greatly based on how they were raised by and the type of parents that they have had. I treat my children with love and respect and hope to bestow great character and good morale in them, so that when they grow up they will have the highest levels of self-esteem, self-worth and confidence. I want them to know that they too can do anything they put their mind to and that they are never less than anyone else.

Childhood development can be influenced not only by what a parent does for their child as well as how they go about doing it, there are studies out there that repeatedly tell of how the way that you were treated as a child can be a direct reflection on how you treat your own children. I make sure that I remind myself of this quite often so that I am different than that study. I can show in how I raise my children that you can overcome your own childhood and make a better one for your own children. I try to make sure that I am never influenced by this character that is supposed to resurface.

Despite the fact that I maintain two to three jobs, I always put my family first before anything, I take my daughter biking, swimming and gymnastics classes and I will do the same for my infant son when he becomes more mobile. I also take my daughter to the gym with me and to work. We wash my car and water our little garden at home together. She absolutely enjoys my presence. I also am sure to read to her at bedtime and help to brush her teeth when she gets up in the morning.

We take care of our own relationship as best as we can, as we have struggled from possibly growing in different directions. Sometimes, I buy her flowers, cards and take her places. Whether it be shopping or on a cruise. I feel it is important for her to realize how much I appreciate her and if for nothing else, giving me my children.

I also have made sure to purchase college savings accounts for them and a life insurance policy on me so that they will have things easier as life goes on. Something I never had the benefit of. The example you set as a parent becomes lodged in that impressionable childhood mind. There it will play a large influence as to how your child sculpts their life as an adult. Who they will be, and who they will strive to become. As a father I will teach my children a positive belief system, how to recognize positive feelings and how to handle the negative things that happen in life. Great value is what they say promotes growth and development in a community. I will teach my children the value of community, how to give without expecting to receive something back in return. I want them to do things because it is the right thing to do, not because of how you could be rewarded in return.

I hope that my children are able to harness the same energy for inspiration as I do. I want them to always be willing to give not only 100% but more like 180% to make sure the job is accomplished, and accomplished well. There is nothing in life that is not achievable, and when you set your mind to do something and to carry it through, it is always important to remember that you complete what you actually set out to do. Sometimes life gets distracting and you need to regroup and focus. But it can be done, and it will be done, by you is a good thing to remind yourself of. I want them to remember to always be humble, and to treat people as you would want to be treated and to always believe in the power above.

Paying it forward

I'VE COME ALONG WAY FROM those days as a boy growing up on Nigeria. I have managed to become involved in a wide array of things that are of interest to me. I currently have volunteered as a personal trainer for those who want to lose weight but are unable to afford a personal trainer. I try to encourage the participants and find the right exercise to help them meet their fitness goals. I am able to monitor their progress and give advice as to how to further progress. I also have served as a soccer coach where I can pass along my knowledge and skills of the sport to younger players through the YMCA soccer program.

I also volunteer within my church, providing security services for the pastor and as a life coach for the community. I feel that if I can overcome everything that I have in my own life that I should be able and willing to influence others that they too can do the same with their own challenges. I have volunteered to also help supervise adolescent troubled youths on probation work towards completing their individual community service commitments in the community.

Volunteering means so much for me as a way to get out there and help people in need that normally wouldn't ask for the help. I have been mentoring at one of the area middle schools and have truly enjoyed every aspect of it. I am also a human rights commissioner at Michigan City Human Rights Commission. There I inquire or intervene in any proceeding involving any allegation of violation of human rights. I have a bright future ahead of me and many more things I would like to accomplish.

I planned this book to teach and educate people on how to persevere. It has long been said that you can do anything if you put your mind into it. In this book you will have learned how to overcome adversity and life obstacles. If you think that you have had it so badly and if you think that you have come to a stop or that you can no longer try anymore because of life changing, by the time you read this book you will have learned that you too can persevere and make the most out of everything that comes to you in life. You will be able to take one more step towards your future being a complete success.

By reading this book you will discover how easy it is to overcome anything that is threatening your happiness. It will change the way you look and feel about temporary life challenges. Whether you are coaching yourself or others or just simply looking for what it takes to make it through and persevere then you will find this book an invaluable resource.

The main reoccurring message throughout my life is the way that I was pushed around and around with no love, and how I overcame that set back without carrying the anger with me to adulthood. I was able to rejuvenate myself with the power of perseverance and a high level of tolerance. At some point in my life I struggled with self-acceptance. Lack of self-acceptance was a result of what I went through in my life. That is how I managed to be submissive to my aunt and uncle and would do anything to please them at the expense of my own personal ambitions. When I was denied what I really wanted in life, and that was an education, by my stepmother and father, those hopes and aspirations were still there for me because I chose to keep them alive. And even though they may have seemed to disappear from my conscious mind. I knew that one day I might be able to arise, activate my ambition and shine on. I still sometimes experience traumatic feelings from my past, however I now have the coping skills to handle the stress. I hope every reader will be able remember that it is your mindset that sets you up for failure, or just as easily for success. You are in control of yourself, you choose and pick what motivates you and what not to let bother you. You control your destiny.

If readers could just take one thing away and I cannot repeat it enough, is how I persevered through the darkest times of my life, despite life threatening adversity that I faced. At any time it would have been easy to just give up. I just couldn't let that happen. Every time I would look back and realize how much further I already was from where I had started. As a little boy, with a dream of getting an education.

I am currently warming up to begin my PhD classes in international policy and hope to one day become a professor at the university. I would love to get into politics and perhaps run for mayor, so that I can make things better for the entire community. Then perhaps one day I will retire and I will return to Nigeria to run for governor of the state where I was raised. I already feel that by writing this book, I have not only helped myself but have hopefully also empowered each and every one of you to look at your lives and start making changes for the better. If you grew up and had a great childhood full of nothing but good times and love, then remember that not everyone is dealt the same hand of cards. You can take your already positive background and go one step further and be an influence in someone's life that hasn't experienced all that goodness. This is your life, be sure to make it an amazing one.

I believe that everyone that reads my journey will be touched as my road has been difficult. I felt it important to tell you my story as nothing is impossible and when you are faced with adversity, anyone can overcome the worst of conditions. Be true to yourself, if you find through your many journeys in life that something is not working, and there is an adjustment to be made. Do not waste time, get it done and move on. Life is short and you need to live it to the fullest in order to be happy first and foremost. Be true to yourself.

And to think that this all began when I was merely a boy with a dream. A dream of becoming educated enough to make a difference everywhere that I go in life. Leaving an impact on everyone that I meet. Proof that a dream can take you anywhere that your heart desires.

Acknowledgement

So MANY WONDERFUL PEOPLE have supported me through this journey of writing my first book. I would like to specifically thank:

GOD, for without his continual spiritual guidance, my book would have never come to life.

My beautiful children, Joy and Osajie, to whom I love and adore and who gave me the inspiration to be the best Father that I can be. Who also are too young to realize, that my book was based on my true events of oppression, whereas my promise to them is that they will never have to face anything similar to what their Father endured.

My Manager, Diana Bridges, who spent many unselfish hours, reviewing and editing the manuscript, as she felt compassion and a yearning to assure my story was told.

Sacha Brittburns, a dedicated friend, who gave of her time so unconditionally and one who's drive was to encourage me to place my story on paper to spread the message to so many, that all things are possible and adversity is only a word as I stepped over all barricades that came my way.

The team of friends behind the scenes, for seeing my potential and making this book a reality.

My publishing company, IUniverse, for their input on the process of perfection.

Jose Santiago, my Brother in Christ, who stands by my side through my processes in life, and an individual whom I will always be proud to call by Brother.

My Heartfelt thanks to each and every one of you, as I love and appreciate the gifts I have been given to be able to share my journey. GOD is so wonderful.